ERASING THE SKY

Laurie Wilcox-Meyer

Erasing the Sky

First Printing

ISBN 978-1-970860-97-9

Cover Photo Credit: Nina Ellis Snoddy

CUTTLEFISH
BOOKS

ACKNOWLEDGEMENTS

Thanks are due to the editors and publishers of the following publications in which present or earlier versions of some included poems previously appeared:

Contemporary Haibun Online; Dawn Returns: Haiku Society of America Members' Anthology 2022; Failed Haiku; #FemkuMag; Had I a Dove: Appalachian Poets on the Helene Floods; Hauling the Tide: Haiku Society of America Members' Anthology 2024; Modern Haiku; Pan Haiku Review; Poets for Science; tsuridoro; and *trash panda.*

"while (bumper-to-bumper)" *won third place in the 2024 H Gene Murtha Senryu Contest and was published in Failed Haiku and Prune Juice in accordance with the contest.*

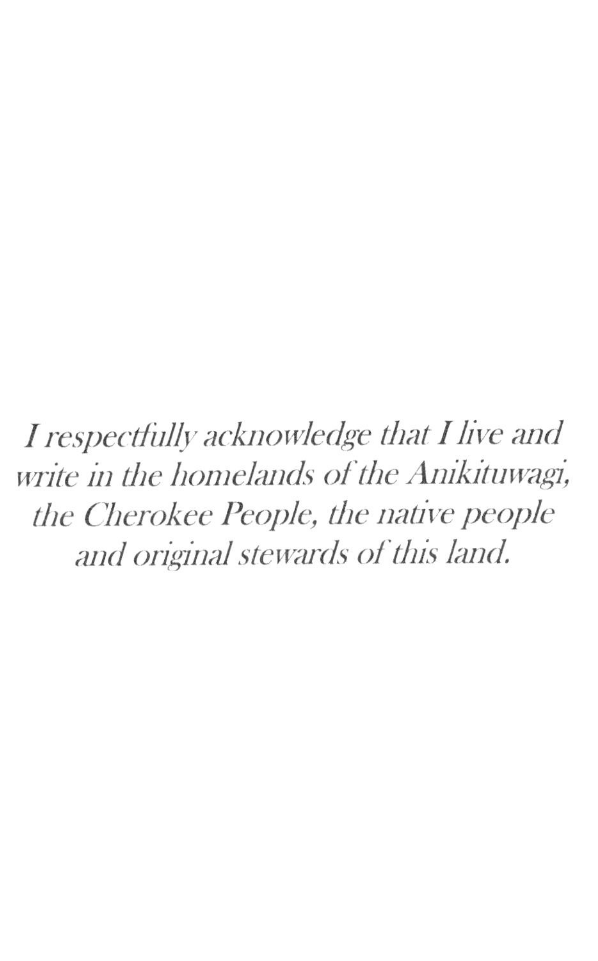

*I respectfully acknowledge that I live and
write in the homelands of the Anikituwagi,
the Cherokee People, the native people
and original stewards of this land.*

ERASING THE SKY

HAIBUN

And a Recent Typhoon
to the Yukon-Kuskokwim Delta

Black bear at my back door, mastodon molars.
In the beginning, one calm eye,
one curious eye. But the righteous ruckus
of chainsaws and jackhammers.

Some of us must choose from dumpsters.
Others remove solar panels from The White House.
Gotta, gotta, gotta set these free?
Greta sails past coastguards and pirates.

The mudslides the floods the wildfires roar.
Yet concrete trucks continue to ooze.
One mother and four cubs forage out back.
It's their yard, these last berries.

     red leaves tapping my window our thirst

Raised by a River

The Tangipahoa River engulfs our tears. Dark eyes
of Katrina envelop most cypress, most bees, homes
with boarded windows. The nameless and named.
Her calm eye flings fledglings too far.

> she laps
> her opponents
> zero-sum game

A knock on my waterlogged back door. Though
my valves barely flutter I fix sandwiches and tea for
another. We rest on once live oak, two chairs. As if
the trunks were still rooted. As if a gator snapped
shut and the turtle swam free.

They Run the World

"The truth is that we need invertebrates
but they don't need us."
—E.O. Wilson

Was taught to fear   spiders   but now i don't

kill them.

      Snakes and toads

                near Rattlesnake Lodge

    still go hungry. We can't live

                without insects

and arachnids. Nowtheclockticksfaster.

        evening pastels...
          camellias
             dropping petals

Tangipahoa River
One Thousand Years From Now

Did you know you've transformed from a dead river
into magical woodlands enveloped in color?
Dying waters of petrochemical foam
phoenixed from wicked waste,
oil and grime, the fires.
No longer victim of gaudy, green dollars.
Vultures to once poisoned deer
now roots, trunks and crowns,
the green mansions entwined.
Copperheads, cottonmouths, and rattlers
no longer the humans with venom.
Once coffined in sludge, herons and songbirds
also wing higher.
Supple ferns of countless spores caress
holy ground. Your wilderness,
a rainbow of praise.
More than a city on a hill.

        Ouachita river...
        a leaf floats by
        in no time

Rattling Helene

The hurricane jolts my house at 5 a.m. Coffee maker silenced. Grandmother's linens speak from a shook attic, Wipe the slate clean. Love floods back, tinged with cruel sadness. Gran would always say she lived too long. Wipe the slate clean. River's susurrus crushed by force. The Earth is bawling.

> not one calm eye. . .
> tractor-trailer under pines
> and oak trunk on the roof

Hurricane Remains

Electrical lines and telephone poles dead on ground. On this walk, it's your rings that beckon. Blue sky and rain within these circles, the years. Intimacy intact yet soon for decay. Roots point toward the stars. Where did we first go astray?

> wooden vase
> on the table
> worn beauty

Circling

She eats from her garden. Protecting its tiny chick splayed on ground a crow dive-bombs my friend. I walk the serpentine labyrinth.

> of rain
> the seeds
> from rain

Nursery Ground

Eddies of plastics and foam. Turgid whirlpools churn to swallow, to swallow again. Wind and rain had gone mad. Rent trees coffin their innards. Because we slept for one too many decades.

five on a roof
the air also flooded

In Louisiana, the delta nursery tends crayfish, shrimp, oysters. Those most humble near dark-ooze whisper have mercy to engineers.

Bonnet Carre spillway:
gray water
forever gray?

After reading a heroine myth to my grandsons we pack up to wander a trail. Wild iris and trillium glow. Yet we talk of monsters on rough seas. One hundred foot waves.

in a small boat, each of us a life buoy

They Always Move Gently

like lacebark elm pulse supple leaves while doves
whisper. Or fireflies' lit intimacy before the fall and
the too-hot sun is tucked away.

> on wire
> bluebirds at ease...
> we tightrope ourselves

Exponential

The cellphone keeps him on leash while he's walking his dog Scout. Perhaps Siri will run a red light or spill his coffee as he drives to work. After long hours at the computer, microchip running shoes tell him how far and fast. Spheres of relentless data like one hundred cups of espresso in overdrive. Will the Goldberg Variations, The Tracks of My Tears and Come Together survive?

> car radio blares
> volume button not found
> these hands are tied

Flung

She forgets her helmet at the office. Head pounds an American sidewalk. Days of darkness. She wakes speaking with an Irish accent. Stroke of insight. Touch of grace.

while (earth is mined open) the plover flies free

It Seems We Need Help

Many used to think of whales as monsters. Does anyone still believe because root vegetables grow toward hell that they shouldn't be eaten? Angels and devils aside, nowadays carrots and beets could be protesting what humans do, after all.

> lighthouse moon
> beams for my dream...
> friend or foe?

A change for the best: Smoking's not allowed on planes. Achoo. Yet progressing slower than snails we're in step with sand crab's backward gait. So where do we go from here and is here even here. Calling all god particles to get us out of this mess. Another achoo.

Parrotfish Speaks

A mucus bubble oozes from my mouth and swaddles me into night. Clever ancestors also keep me safe amid parasites. During the day I rasp coral to gather algae. Diversity still blooms. Water's pressure is no pressure at all. My rough lips smack the ocean of love. Hormones gush a rainbow of color.

> a coral necklace
> gift wrapped
> more is less in this case

On Edge

I dash to get done what (I think) has to be done. Have scurried to post offices in raging thunderstorms. (Not without a speeding ticket.) Projects and hurdles, a state bottle bill didn't get passed though we were fierce. The devil's details tick-tock without end, leading where?

> at the gas station
> one humorous sign:
> .59/lb boneless bananas

A Buddhist monk next to me on a plane once shared: Feeling pressured is no sin. Then he cringed as turbulence jolted him closer to me.

my mother at 90 leaves her phone off the hook

Unfurling

Side by side by side on yoga mats.
This golden glow swaddles me.
Like the cathedral of live oaks—
    I have been before.

Now, a yellow scarf the sun's rays.
Batik-cotton-bolsters the rich soil.
Eastern chants wave on—
    Our roots entwine.

        buds once closed—
        quiet ground speaks
        of an open lotus

HAIKU & SENRYU

protests downtown
a bluebird listens

sardines
in mass migration
american fear

a congress of crow erasing the sky

asking for plastic bags
at the grocery
last night's nightmare

more white houses,
fewer trees—
a caution of wind

peeling beets
the stains on my cold skin...
the blood on our hands

these potatoes
tastealien
PFAS invasion

to-save list
ten feet long
florida manatee...

eels migrate
across the atlantic
living the question

this cast...
a stone's skip
into sunset

while (bumper-to-bumper) the willow sways

the hawk flapping
near circling vultures—
arrhythmia

sturdy vine
on the aging oak
our union

birdsong
high in the trees...
earth's vibrato

the ant on my deck
carries a sliver of cheese
the strength of one

mice—
they may
or may not be here

morning meditation...
beyond the brook
a deeper spring

garlic wafts in church holy ghost

i commune
with this day
wafer moon

waterfall...
never wed
to my watch

kerfed oak
gray grief
returns

two hawks
glide
the gloaming

driftwood on the beach
tides
in the trees

blue heron
of first light
her last breath

chinese forget-me-not how blue the unmarked grave

evening meditation...
the hours melt
into pastels

chrysalis
on the lawn chair...
evening breeze

hummingbird zings
flower to flower
her quips

crows bobbing
their yes's
i agree

the dazzle of zebra
a more perfect
union

mammatus clouds manna they never had

sourwood trunk...
the railroad tracks
leading home

osprey with fish
in tow
the weight of the world

ABOUT THE AUTHOR

Laurie Wilcox-Meyer's third poetry collection, *Conversation In The Key Of Blue*, was published by Main Street Rag Publishing, 2020. She lives in the French Broad River basin in the Blue Ridge Mountains of North Carolina where she often spots bears while hiking and meditating about her next poem. Her poetry is also shaped by her upbringing in Louisiana, where she played Chopin and dodged alligators while waterskiing. *Though the Warbler Sings*, a collection of 68 poems, will be published by Finishing Line Press in August, 2026.